Silence

Silence, a collection of poems + quotes
Copyright © 2021 by Michelle Renae

All rights reserved. No part of this book may be reproduced in any manner whatsoever without written permission from the author.

First Printing, 2021

ISBN 978-1-7342611-0-3

Cover design and words by Michelle Renae

www.michellerenae.com
Follow along on Instagram @michellerenaewriter

To all the dreamers, the lovers and
the wandering souls.

Silence

A Collection of Poems + Quotes

Michelle Renae

I write for the wounded
and the bleeding hearts
I know what it is to break
to return, again and again
pieces half mended
barely holding on
I write for the mournful
buried in grief until the
bones ache and
the heart *atrophies*
I feel what you've become
despite the years spent
clawing through the soil
of despair
Somehow unscathed and unburdened
by life's poor attempt to steal
the light from your precious soul

xo
Michelle Renae

LEAVING

MICHELLE RENAE

I didn't know it was possible
to feel alone in your presence
an *afterthought*
Insignificant to you life's agenda
So, I had to leave to create my own.

SILENCE

the one i miss the most
is the me
I couldn't be
when I was with you

MICHELLE RENAE

No tears
meant the
start
of the end
of my life
lived for him.

SILENCE

"Sometimes *exiting* is the only strategy."

MICHELLE RENAE

I can't do this anymore.
*- five words to
end a marriage*

SILENCE

all it took was a second
a moment of rage
to inspire you
to try and
take my life
your bare hands
clenched around my throat
bruises left
where your desperation began.
   - closure

MICHELLE RENAE

Desperation knows
no bounds
when there is
nothing left to lose.

SILENCE

It was not a man
I witnessed
but a wounded animal
    wrought with fear
lunging
snarling
spiraling....out of control
Unaware that his coming apart
could not undo the
destruction that
had already been done.

MICHELLE RENAE

"Even in the cracks,
wildflowers grow
defiant like my
     untamed heart."

SILENCE

Call me heartless
But I don't wonder how you are
Any thought of you leaves me reeling
With *regrets*
How young and naïve I was then
      You willingly stole away my youth
and I blindly let you rob me

MICHELLE RENAE

The best part of
being me
is never having to
answer to you.

SILENCE

He made it easier and
easier to leave.
Years spent locked away
in someone else's dream.

Settled, but discontent.
Ravaged by an aching to
break loose from
the grip of a *common life*

MICHELLE RENAE

She's gone.
No trace left behind of
    her insignificance.
A kind of beautifully
staged death.
The casualty of insecurity.
and hopeless romanticism.
Just a stranger that shares my
shadow who barely warrants
a memory now.

SILENCE

Grateful for the breaking
For the words that
Painted doubt in my mind
Grateful for your insecurities
That pushed mine to the surface
Grateful you stole
the best years of my life
So, I could become
    the woman I am today
Grateful for the courage
to leave you behind
Grateful for all the adventures
I've had without you
The lips I've kissed that weren't yours
Grateful for the end
So, I could begin... again

   - thank you

MICHELLE RENAE

Your cruelty underneath that
smiling facade
wore clean my conscious
of leaving you behind.

SILENCE

Took me years
to repair the damage
you left behind with your
poisonous tongue
10,000 lashes of emotional
destruction
from your insecure lips

   - you can't take it back

MICHELLE RENAE

You must have caught a glimpse
The way a hawk sees the
shimmer of its prey
glistening under the
water's surface
Unaware that swimming
in the shallows
could be so deadly
You must have seen it
long before she did
A young heart who had
yet to taste the world
Her fierce hunger
and mad passion for life
You kept it to yourself
Feared the discovery of it all
might upset your vision of
what was supposed to be
Feared the day her wings
would replace her insecurities
and she'd take flight

- and she did

SILENCE

I never fully realized
The courage it took
To leave a toxic relationship
    I thought it would be simple

Like leaving the party unnoticed
Surely, I wouldn't be missed
No harm done

But, it was no leisurely stroll
along the beach
with a sunset
or saltwater kisses
goodbye

It was a strenuous hike
through the
lifeless landscape
of a crumbling canyon

Whose walls started
to close in
violent
    volatile
unstable and harsh

    - leaving did not go as planned

MICHELLE RENAE

Your insecurities
Became the *fuel* I needed
To finally let you go

SILENCE

death hovered over me
like a long-lost friend
comforted me through
the endless sobs

my image reflected back to me
when I finally gave in
I swallowed down the emptiness
with a bottle of wine

closed my eyes
never intending to wake
death let me lie down
in my tears

he held my hand
patient
ever watchful
a *silence* fell over me

hours passed without warning
until the sun pierced through the blinds
oblivious to the darkness and forced me to
see another day

- it wasn't my time

LOVING

MICHELLE RENAE

Calling me
sugar
melts me
down like
gold on fire.

SILENCE

Your love was a narcotic
I failed to come clean from
Suffered withdrawals and
Seclusion
     I fell into *madness*
Years couldn't wash away
the addiction of your
skin against mine

MICHELLE RENAE

Drunk and in love
sounds like a
pretty good
way to spend the
night with you.

SILENCE

One look from you tilts
    the *Earth* on its axis

MICHELLE RENAE

timing was never a
friend to us
she couldn't be trusted
let us slip through
her deceit without remorse
we emerged from the
depths over and over
despite her clever attempts
to keep us apart
here we are years later
but we can never cross her
once again, she has us
waiting in the dark

SILENCE

I'm caught in a
daydream
about
the what ifs
could haves
should have been
and all I'm
left with at
the end
of the
hour is a
never will be

MICHELLE RENAE

There was a moment
when I recognized
I was a willing participant
in some kind of
                madness.
A madness that had
devoured me whole and
hovered somewhere between
love and total dysfunction.

SILENCE

Like two little children
caught playing with matches.
Neither of us knowing how much we
        could burn with our young, ***wild hearts***

MICHELLE RENAE

Of all the places
I've been
Your *heart*
was never
one of them

SILENCE

I wonder how long you'll
inject yourself into my life
Unsolicited
Unexpected
      Out of the blue
Just when I've gotten to a place
Of rarely thinking of you
Rarely dreaming of you
There you are once again
      A painful scar that just
won't fade away

MICHELLE RENAE

Darling,
I want
to hear your
long stories.
Don't you see?
When you speak,
my *heart* expands
and your words
become the
air I breathe.

SILENCE

Two strangers
who used to
be lovers
now trying to
be friends

- this won't work

MICHELLE RENAE

Two souls who
    traveled
the stars
and heavens to
join the journey
of forever
here on Earth.

- a cosmic love

SILENCE

Naive is the heart
that after years of breaking
suffers *amnesia*
at the sight of you.

MICHELLE RENAE

Letting go
doesn't mean
forgetting
It just means
I'm finally at
peace
and that's the only
closure
I'll ever need

SILENCE

Your leaving was a
glacier calving
into the sea.
Massive, cold and
      heartbreaking.

MICHELLE RENAE

loving you in
my dreams
has become my
    living nightmare.

SILENCE

Drifting aimlessly
    drowning in your *silence*.
Capsized.
Traumatized.
Waiting for a reason
the tide will pull me
back to shore.
For saltwater to cleanse my
skin of your memory.
I beg Death not to
let me slip through his
fingers this time.
Leaving me lost in the dark
shallow waves forever.

MICHELLE RENAE

Want to take a
razor to this
cord that keeps us bound.
The split ends
of a love torn
apart by space and time.
Always stuck in a gray abyss
where yes or no
doesn't exist.
Just this empty
void of a "maybe"
holding on for dear life.

SILENCE

You haunt me
in my dreams
like a wolf
stalking its prey.
Slow.
Steady.
Calculating.
My heart beat
pulsing the closer
your body gets to mine.
You lunge toward me
and I'm transfixed
I lay motionless
until I die...
every time I wake

MICHELLE RENAE

"Sometimes the
wounds of love
exist without an
expiration date."

SILENCE

I want to walk the streets with you
in the dead of night
Hand in hand
Side by side
Want to kiss your joy and
steal your laughter until all that
is left is a love story
That can only be told when
we're old and gray

- To the man I haven't met yet

MICHELLE RENAE

It feels like it's taken me a lifetime
to come to terms with the
colossal *emptiness* you left behind
        a hole the size of the moon itself
gaping and unwilling to close
for fear of having to live a life where you
don't exist even if it's just in my mind

SILENCE

I never knew
there were a
million and one
ways to write of
a *broken heart*.
But, then I never
knew there were a
million and one
ways to break one.

MICHELLE RENAE

The wicked way in
which time creates
space a million miles wide
and passion sits
a centimeter from never
What a cruel irony
to be so close yet so
tragically far away.

- greeting an old lover

SILENCE

A little piece of me
will always want a
little piece of
you

MICHELLE RENAE

Wishing never could
Turn you into the
Man I deserved
And wishing
Never could make up
For what should have been
And wishing never could keep
You from my dreams
And wishing never could
Make you stay

   - I wish

SILENCE

he was a glass of wine
on a warm sunny day
a buzz of sweetness on the lips

   - a feeling I did not want to part with

MICHELLE RENAE

Please refrain from
loving me so much.
Your smile and warmth
are comfort
a worn sweater wrapped
around me.
You hold me captive
with your kiss
and I am dazed.
Please don't let me wake
if loving you is
just a *dream*.

SILENCE

I have grieved our love
for years
Written things I will
never say to you
Felt you in far
off places I've traveled to alone
Been desperate to
share with you
all the experiences
we will never have
Nothing but a
futile existence in
loving

Michelle Renae

I remember a time
When love felt easy
I welcomed it with arms
wide open
But, over the years as
unavailable
crept in
time and time again
my heart lost interest in
the maybe and
the might have been

SILENCE

You gave me
no choice
but to live with this
restructured organ.
How could something so
    vital become so *mutilated?*
A half beating heart
left for dead by
your absence.

MICHELLE RENAE

Loving me
Will only
cost your soul
in return

- maybe the price is too high

SILENCE

He was the kind of man
who could
make me forget
what I was saying
mid-sentence
Fall drunk and in love
Meet me at midnight
    Get us kicked out of a cab
with our indecency
Kiss my hand to tell me
he missed me
Talk about everything
and nothing
    naked on a Sunday morning
A trained assassin
Who killed me with his
silent goodbye

MICHELLE RENAE

Your taking was
A gift
I never intend to repay

   - I'm a better woman

SILENCE

Guess you didn't
understand
I'm a woman with armor
Hold close all the
things I can't say
If I gave you a whisper
of doubt
that was not my intention
When I laid bare my soul
you mistook my courage
for weakness
Oh and now darling,
look what we've lost
An *almost love* is all
that remains

MICHELLE RENAE

I'd like to hang on to
the memory of you
Just a little longer
Even if it's just to fill
my heart with your
expired kisses
and the feeling of
your hand in mine
Strolling through a museum
on a Saturday afternoon

- history

SILENCE

I find it difficult to explain
the way my heart
silently shuts down
no sound or warning
no fuss
a beautiful preservation
from a lover's careless words
no anger
just a quiet sadness and a
shallow breath of
disappointment

MICHELLE RENAE

Of all the
directions
our love could
have traveled,
 sideways
was never what
I imagined.

SILENCE

I wish I could tell you
what's in my heart and
on my mind
But, for now my
kisses
will have to do.

xx

MICHELLE RENAE

I try not to curse under my breath
those early morning memories
dreams I've woken from
that bare your face
my lips whispering your name
like it was yesterday
Seems pointless to try and forget you
when the architects of my mind
        are hell-bent on
skillfully building you back into
my life
every time I close my eyes

SILENCE

"There is a courage in
having *feelings*
and a courage in walking away
despite them."

MICHELLE RENAE

I've grown weary and
my patience worn thin
from the carelessness of men
who want to share my bed
    but not *my dreams*
unable to tame this woman in all her power
lighting up the dark spaces
they keep hidden
...a terror cloaked in beautiful flesh
and long brown hair.

SILENCE

"Bitterness
is a pill I'm trying
not to choke on"

MICHELLE RENAE

Every time I talk
myself out of liking
you too much
You go and do
something sweet
Like call me
just to hear my voice
When yours is
too tired to speak

SILENCE

He was the sin I couldn't
wipe clean
A mark of lust embedded
into my skin
Like a tattoo forever
staining my heart
Existing on borrowed time
      the devil stole from me
And now it feels like just
a dream I'll never wake from
In a world we worked
hard to escape
Two lovers
hand in hand
Walking over the edge
into oblivion

MICHELLE RENAE

I never knew that one long
exhale
could carry the weight
of a thousand goodbyes.

SILENCE

My last tear has made its way
down my disheartened face
Your name no longer touches
the tip of my tongue in
quiet desperation
My heart is in *atrophy*
Void of the thought of a
you and a me
of a maybe
a someday
My skin has finally shed
the memory of yours against mine
and I'm grateful for this end
So I can begin
To love myself...again

MICHELLE RENAE

I walk around
forever holding my peace
An emptiness surrounds me
trying to make sense of
the loss of us
of this place
it holds pieces of our past
and all directional signs
point to you
i walk around
while memories stain my heart and
tears fill the cracks in the sidewalk

- a trip down memory lane

SILENCE

I no longer
have
space
for your
indecision.

MICHELLE RENAE

If we look up
to the night sky
do you think we could
meet each other
where the big dipper lines up
with the little one?

- star-crossed lovers

SILENCE

I imagine with such severity
That he's out there
Searching
    Wandering
Taking it all in
A sense of polarity in his heart
Seeking an unattainable truth
In the dream
Of passion and desire
For another wandering soul
whose will is broken
at the sight of him

- my other half is looking for me too

MICHELLE RENAE

Not sure there will ever be
a better feeling
than your arms wrapped
around my shoulders
your head leaning against mine
signaling
I'm yours in a crowded room

SILENCE

"They say happiness
is a choice
But how can
I choose to see
the *bright side*
in your absence"

MICHELLE RENAE

You are the poetry I long
to write
A man keen to change
my mind about love
My escape from the ordinary and
the uncommitted
Or maybe *a lifeline* from
the boat where I stand sinking
A blunt force trauma to the heart
and the cry of a woman
who has been drowning
in sorrow for
far too long

SILENCE

I dreamt about you
again last night
Seems no amount of
mental fist fighting
can rid you from my thoughts
Exhausted from the false reality
of your hand in mine
Walking around places we've never been
Loving each other like no time has passed
    A punch to the soul
leaving me bloodied and bruised
drained and worn out
Waking to find it was nothing
more than a figment of my
imagination...once again

- I'm tired even when I sleep

LIVING

MICHELLE RENAE

I raise a glass
to you
to love
    to life
to fear
For all the Hail Mary's
and the Holy hells
What an adventure this has been to be sure
Champagne could never quite
rise to the occasion of celebration
for this miracle in living
But, I'll drink it down
with a grin and a happy heart

SILENCE

"We are all trying to
carve sculptures in a
garden full of souls"

MICHELLE RENAE

I stood among the
towering giants
Limbs stretched out like
long lost friends
A moss-covered floor
of wildflowers and stone
greeted me with their beauty
      How long had I been
      holding my breath?
All at once, my chest heaved as
tears of grief
flowed down to water the Earth
Unaware of my
own deprivation from the only
place I know that
feels like home.

  - *nature is the only place I feel at home*

SILENCE

I must have tripped
somewhere along the way
my path diverted
by accident
guess it simply
went unnoticed
because, where I
stand now
feels like a
    thousand miles
from anywhere I
should really be

  - a bit lost

MICHELLE RENAE

Stretch your
heart to the dark
sky and
whisper your
sweet nothings.
Half-light or
full light,
the *Moon*
listens without
shying away.

SILENCE

I'm happy living an
untamed life
A loose kind of love
for the taste of
uncertainty

MICHELLE RENAE

Seems that little spark of
love
joy
and
laughter
has been playing
hide-and-seek
I count to ten and go
about my day
But...
I'm losing the game

SILENCE

I fumble my way
through the words
a *delicate undertaking*
for a sensitive soul
to find a way to speak
without saying a thing

MICHELLE RENAE

"There is a sadness to you", he said
How could there not be?

All of these little
life tragedies
not little at all
Colossal
Taking up space
hardly leaving room for
happiness to reside

 - *no vacancy*

SILENCE

I carry burdens
of the future
Regrets of the past
While longing for
the *present*

MICHELLE RENAE

I'm often caught
in a trap
of seeing the best in
others
while I suffer the
wounds of
future regret.

SILENCE

The cracks in the pavement
weep under the weight
of our carelessness
silent apathy
gives way to bloodshed
and grief
for a life we've only imagined
but cannot commit for fear of change
our hearts no longer caring for the innocent
    living in a free world bound by
years of
self-interest and unrest

-wishing for a better world

MICHELLE RENAE

All I want to do is
write
about you
about us
about life
about love
about everything
and *nothing at all*

SILENCE

I don't know about you,
but I could use a little
__more love__
and a lot more wine.

MICHELLE RENAE

She whispers to me
miles from any shoreline
    Her treacherous beauty
and infamy of unpredictability
The way she controls
life above and below
Strong enough to tug at
    the hearts of men
Soft enough to tempt
a woman's soul

- the ocean is calling

SILENCE

I have remained silent for too long
Impatiently waiting for this
melancholy muse to reveal herself
Instead, I wasted the dark hours
hoping
wishing
    begging
for her to surface
to move my pen across the page
in perfect motion
A love/hate relationship gave way
to my unhappy mood
A longing to write of the wounds
that only my words can heal

- writers block

MICHELLE RENAE

Take a deep breath,
my love
All this waiting and
bitter impatience has a
purpose
Time has a way of
   testing us
If you surrender,
your heart will be grateful
it passed

SILENCE

I'm giving up the fight
my hands are bruised
and my heart remains beaten
the cuts have made their way
deep into my soul and
I've had enough now
of pretending that I fit in at all
where round things reside and
clearly my shape was always
meant to be square

- square peg, round hole

MICHELLE RENAE

"Let your heart
crack open with
joy for the
possibility
of what can be."

SILENCE

The mind is such a
beautiful thing
To dream of places
you've never been
Love people you've
never met
What an incredible world
it creates when you
close your eyes
Even if it means
keeping you in the dark
Just so you can see
the light

MICHELLE RENAE

There is a beauty in
being broken
A precious artifact…
your cracks fused
with gold
Mended back into
imperfection
Remaining priceless to
all who hold you close.

SILENCE

I want to sit at my
vintage desk made from an
old bowling alley lane
Type feverishly away on my
antique typewriter until my
fingers blister and bleed
Not enough hours in the day
to sustain my lust for words
Thoughts that have been
held captive far too long
Escaping on paper seems
to be the only remedy
for my *wild mind*

MICHELLE RENAE

I've grown resentful
of this anchor of
responsibility that
    drags me through
the passing hours
of the day
it leaves me suffocated
heavy with longing
for a new horizon

SILENCE

I worry that
one day the
ghosts I've kept
hidden in the
dark alleys of
my mind
will creep along
through the grime
and leave a
permanent residue
of regret
that I've so
carefully evaded
with a fake grin
and a bottle of wine.

MICHELLE RENAE

I am filled with fear
of missing all the
places I have never been
Things I haven't tried
Lips I haven't kissed
What is life, if not
a novel of
never-ending
adventures and love?
Unwritten pages
screaming out for
spilled ink to
form this book
of being human.

SILENCE

Dearest one,
It's okay to
grieve for the life
you had
imagined.
The lost loves
missed opportunities
close calls
the chances you
didn't take.
But, what a gift
just to live life
even if it's
all in your imagination.

MICHELLE RENAE

"Self-preservation
is the
promise
of a
lonely life."

SILENCE

grief crept in
a pest in the night
  silent
unannounced
an unwelcome guest
with no room to move in
but it pushed aside the
pieces of my mind
made itself at home
settled in the cracks
tore at the walls
filled the rooms
with despair
a melancholy that
couldn't be evicted
wishing
waiting
hoping
it would starve itself
and become scarce

MICHELLE RENAE

My mind wanders
through the
concrete jungle.
The ultimate trap of
domestication.
Breaking free of
societal constraints
is the only
obsession.
A caged animal pacing
in a tight space -
suffering from
mental fatigue,
resentment
and soul crushing
defeat.

   - adulting

SILENCE

They lay wilted on the table
Devoid of life or purpose
One touch of my hand and
Everything will crumble
Once living in glorious beauty
Have now shriveled to nothing
For temporary display
How small a life
That all at once
Is cut short of breath,
water and sunlight

- somedays I'm the bouquet

MICHELLE RENAE

These daily grinds
leave nothing in my
heart for desire
I only feel content
when I dash out into
the world I wish to create
Leaving ripples of
nervous laughter in my wake
The uncertainty of it all
my only comfort
Anything else is a blatant
disregard for my well-being.

- driven by curiosity

SILENCE

I desire a man
I desire
who desires me
and my appetite for
adventure.

MICHELLE RENAE

What if
words never written
could never be spoken
never be felt
heard from another
What if
hearts never healed
wounds never closed
noise never silenced
What if
chaos had a home
never welcomed
lies never told
truths never heard
What if
kindness held your hand
never let go
What if
forgiveness strangled
your mind
held a grudge
What if
breathing was hard
and *loving was easy*

SILENCE

I've betrayed myself
Too long spent in
concrete
Void of the splendor of
walking among the trees
My ears tuned into
a bird song,
a hum of the bee
hard at work
Rays of sunlight
desperate to reach
the wildflowers
whose time has
come to bloom.

MICHELLE RENAE

You don't know when it happened exactly
The moment you realized your
heart gave way
Cleared a path
To the unconditional
The unexpected
Late nights and early mornings
when you preferred to sleep in
A smile for the tiniest nudge or the funniest antic
you never knew you missed until now
Your world becomes disrupted by the
 sweetest of
    creations
You didn't stand a chance with a love so pure
Now you receive far more than you could ever give
Just a hope that for even the briefest of time,
you gave a life a loving home

  - a dog's love

SILENCE

there is a calling
a soft whisper of desire
for time spent in the wild
to bask in the morning light
that touches the flowers
on the cold, damp Earth
like fingers dragging across
the small of my back
    awakened senses
a moment when all that
went dark and still
is born again
for the world to see

MICHELLE RENAE

Have I always
    been this *restless?*
An insatiable curiosity for
life
love
learning
growing
moving
changing
On the days I am feeling lost,
I remind myself that being
driven by uncertainty is
embedded deep into
my wandering bones.

SILENCE

"Every time I
venture out in the
wilderness
it's like greeting an
old friend - this sort of
warm feeling of
being home."

MICHELLE RENAE

Let's walk together
hand in hand
along a cool morning
and listen to the
birds singing
to tell the others
they've made it through the night
There's a beauty in their
resurgence
don't you think?
A sort of proud proclamation
That they've made it
through the dark to
see another day

SILENCE

How can the Moon,
the very thing
I've seen a thousand times,
still take my breathe away
when she rises?
A radiant light in
      the darkness of humanity.
A keeper of secrets
from years past.
Her presence so powerful
she controls the tides.

MICHELLE RENAE

I'm so torn
between the woman
I want to be
and the woman
I am

 - *tug-o-war*

SILENCE

I feel my heart crack
A log split in two
Splinters strewn
across the morning fog
A mystery in waiting
Quietly questioning
the time it might take
to piece it back together

MICHELLE RENAE

we are all
stardust
shimmering flecks
of *color and light*
desperate to
break free
of the darkness

SILENCE

I always knew time
was a *tricky little thing*
an illusion
unforgiving
always sneaking around
behind my back
Leading me
on
and on
...until it slipped through
my fingers
and I never even
noticed it was gone

MICHELLE RENAE

A flower never
asks permission
to *bloom and grow*
Why, then darling,
would you?

SILENCE

dream fearlessly,
my love
hold tight those
desires
expectations
ambitions
in your heart
when the sun kisses the sky
it does so with all the certainty
of a new dawn
no questions
no doubts
so, when morning comes for us
be ready to put gratitude to life
and thank those stars that let
the light shine on another day

- you got this

Thank you for choosing to read my work and for following along on this wild ride of creative expression! It means the world to me.

I never intended to write poetry, but it found its way into my soul. I tried desperately to break up with it. More times than I can count. But, each day the call kept getting louder and louder until I finally gave in. It's as if someone else has taken over the movement of my pen when I write and I become the grateful vessel and a willing bystander.

I do believe words have the power to inspire, entertain, impact and enlighten. They give you a glimpse into the creators' heart and soul. I hope my work has done that and also provided a glimmer of hope, love and a spark that moves you.

Love, Peace + Poetry,

Michelle Renae

www.ingramcontent.com/pod-product-compliance
Lightning Source LLC
Chambersburg PA
CBHW052206090526
44583CB00017BA/2350